the falling,
the becoming

CHARLOTTE L OAKEBY

To the girl I used to be,
From the woman I am becoming

contents

i fell in love with your words
that was it
transient spells spelt by your lips

now as i write
i fall in love with my own

—*i am the love of my own life*

an open love letter

      this is an open love letter to whoever reads it. let my words kiss you, soothe you, tell you that *everything will fall into place* one of these days. my love letters never lie.

      i started writing a week after the breakup. the pages you hold in your hands are the whispers of my hurting heart. please be kind to her. in eighteen years of life, i lost my father, my first love, and through that, myself. penning this collection is my way of closing the chapter in which i found the untouched, transient beauty of falling in love for the first time. when i lost him, i lost whatever was left of my teenage naivety. and with it went *the dream*.

      this is a collection of poetry and short fiction about love and the loss of it, written by a lovesick romantic who will fall so helplessly back into love's arms, time and time again, even when it doesn't want to catch her. i am in love with being in love.

      my writing uses a blend of literary styles, from loving, soppy sonnets to dark, bitter fiction. i am heavily inspired by the romantics, confessional poetry, greek mythology and the noir genre. for the first time, quite possibly, i reject a cover of beauty to pacify the pain of my deepest spells. i refuse to shy away from the darkest truths of this mad world, as much as i refuse to ignore the sublimity of its prettiest lies and fantasies. this is first love. this is the fallout. this is the falling, the becoming.

      i am nineteen. i have much more to learn, explore and figure out than i once thought. to convince myself that i am immune from such pain for the rest of my existence would be a circumnavigation of the known rules of the human condition.

no matter how many times he told me to just let go, my heart would not, and so i let her stay a little longer. booked her in for a few extra months at the heartbreak hotel. during our stayover, i listened to her. i sowed seeds within the cracks of her brokenness and let them blossom into blessings. i trusted the clock would fix us. i learnt there is no garden without a little devil's ivy. and then, i found out for myself that the rose does not bloom overnight. patience. that is key.

i'm trusting you with the most delicate part of my heart, for i hurt on these pages but heal within the covers. come inside my fairytale. bathe in the beauty of our love's delusions. i want this book to be a magic potion for those who just need a sip of something. i cannot wait to share my heart with the world.

fall in love with yourself before you let someone share it with you.

the falling

Heaven Lost

A heaven lost and now we fall.
Far better days than in that place,
For what we lost was no heaven at all.

How can it be, Jove's tragic call,
A soft descent and sweet disgrace?
A heaven lost and now we fall.

Our life-sworn love now twisted drawl.
Hell's searing flames, they kiss and grace,
For what we lost was no heaven at all.

The nether's dusk does me enthral.
Oh, how it burns, our scorchèd trace!
A heaven lost and now we fall.

The string that binds us devil-pulled,
We plummet down towards their base,
For what we lost was no heaven at all.

Far from the days of cruel love's thrall,
We hurtle through this tempting space.
A heaven lost and now we fall,
For what we lost was no heaven at all.

countless tear-stained
tickets stashed in locked
boxes remind me of the ones
i've loved, starry-eyed, then
always lost
for so much of my life
has been a movie with the
same sorry plot
and for once
i want to play someone
other than myself
—*i'm so tired of it all.*
no wonder it feels like
they've walked onto a set
when they enter my life
—enter stage right!
—just love me like this!
—then love me like that!
yet fifteen minutes never
turns into a night and so
i cast them as they come
fresh script for every lover
new ways to spoil my ending
(make me want it a little faster)
since i'm sick of these breaks
i've had enough of this show
if you've nothing left to show me
i don't want you anymore
—exit stage door right

cut.
i'd like to go again!

—*the sorrow of a starlet*

Would you have picked him in a crowded room?

Oh, dearest one, if I had
that sort of emotional awareness I
would never have walked into the room
in the first place.

—*to be read in a regretful tone*

Forever Yours, Mr. Carter

Revised Edition
Previously published in Volume 13 of Cosumnes River Journal,
Sacramento, California, May 2019

It's him. It has to be him. I recognise the back of his tousled hair, its tips brushing gently against the collar of his crisp, white shirt. I hear the chime of laughter escape his lips, letting it charm me, and see the way he adjusts his tie, whilst swirling bloodied wine around the glass he holds so carefully between his fingertips. I can picture the confidence oozing through the veins that snake underneath his skin, as he captures the attention of the Bambi-eyed female who sits opposite him. Her blue eyes are lined with black kohl and misted over in awe, her gaze fixated on the stubble scattered over his chin. She falls helplessly into the sunken dimples of his cheeks. I remember how they caught me. I know it's him. It's Christian Carter.

My eyes are roaring flames, dancing and flitting around my surroundings. I don't fit in here, slumped on this bar stool, with my tangled hair and unflattering tracksuit. I glance half-heartedly at the several empty glasses gathered around me, and then trace my finger in and out of the wooden grooves of the table. The drink has already risen to my head. I told myself not to do this tonight.

'Can I get you another?' the boyish barman asks me in his lively tone, just as usual, grabbing the pint glasses and clinking them in unison. They sing at me. He doesn't look old enough to be in this pub, let alone manning it, but he still doesn't even try and pretend not to know what my answer will be. It won't be any different from the countless times he's asked me this before. I nod and mumble something under my breath, fumbling in my pocket and pulling out a crumpled fiver.

I can't help but stare at them. I should be sitting there, bathing in pools of his caramel skin, soaking up his musky scent. I bought him that crisp, white shirt. And that tie. I was his everything until everything was gone. I won't leave him alone until I finish what I came to do.

I wrap my fingers around the fresh pint with such force that froth spills over the edge and trickles between my fingers. There's a shuffle of chairs as he helps her put on her jacket, some sort of studded Alexander McQueen, his chest brushing against her buttered curls. One wet peck on the cheek later, and they head to the car park. I follow behind them. This is my chance. I have to take it.

I'm not sure what sickens me more—the sweet tinkles of her giggles, or my excitement. My abandoned beer waits to surprise the barman; another wasted fiver, but to waste this opportunity would be *criminal*. I lurk in the shadows and watch him swing his car keys between stubby fingers, waiting for the slam of his navy BMW doors.

Despite being close to eleven at night, the temperature at the peak of June wraps itself around me like some sort of force field. The remnants of a muggy, unbearable heat lingers in the air, and along with the sour taste of drink on my tongue, I feel frustrated. I hear the rev of Christian's turbo engine—he always was a show off, after all—and the car purrs out of the pub.

He takes us down an everlasting road. I can't

recognise it and my head pounds, my vision becoming nothing more than melted blurs and contorted shapes until the car swerves abruptly and I'm forced to jerk the steering wheel back into control. I've always had a problem with alcohol. It's why Christian left me. I never know when to stop, apparently. That's what he told me after we lost the baby. I push down on the accelerator a little harder.

*

We must've travelled a few miles when I see the orange glow of his rear lights slip into a turning. My foot finds the brake and we slow down, the car's roar hushing to a whisper. A weakly-flickering lantern calls my name, inviting me inside the property's drive. It'd be rude not to accept. Sure enough, the navy BMW is there—in prime position.

Hastily, I open the glove box and rummage in a chaotic mess of rusting coins and empty pill bottles and their papered prescriptions before I find what I'm looking for. I open the car door, inch by inch, and leave it there—it would make too much noise to shut it. I creep towards the BMW, twisting the cap of my tin of lighter fluid, and, using my other hand, slide open my matchbox, staring at the three single matches with dissatisfaction. I'll have to sacrifice my midnight cigarette.

I have one chance to get this right. One chance to get my revenge. He left me when I needed him most. What's more, he blamed it on me. My vices killed the baby, he'd screamed. My damned vices!

To my delight, the backseat window is open slightly, and although I'm immersed in complete darkness, I gently tilt the tin's nozzle into the car and feel the weight of it decreasing as its liquid soaks the interior. I swipe the chosen match against the matchbox and an amber tongue sparks instantly, curling around the wood, devouring it. Without a second thought, I toss it into the car and run towards the safety of my own.

I crouch, feeling the heat of the glorious flame kissing my cheek. A minute later, it's high in the air, a splendid fire, licking up any remains. My eyes burn with the satisfaction of it all. Splendid, splendid fire!

Here we go. The moment I've waited for arrives. The front door swings open, its sniggering silver knocker rattling against the varnished wood. He sprints out, shouting expletives that are silenced by the raging of my fire. Perhaps I should burn his acid tongue next. What an explosion that would be.

I study the devastated look melting onto his face as he watches his beloved four-wheeled, five-doored lover burning to pieces. I soak up every moment of his priceless despair. He's learning how it feels to lose something he loves.

I'm expecting his other lady lover to run after him, tottering in her kitten heels, silk blouse slipping off her shoulder if he hadn't already taken it off. But there's no sign of Bambi-eyes. I think he realises this at the same time as I do, because his gaze turns hollow and meaningless.

Then, I see it. Among the wreckage, I see a charred hand lying on the gravel.

On An Appearance

Raspberry kisses exit
From her lips like ampersands.
Sinful, sinful lips,
Stuck on a guilty mouth
Like a feather-tailed dart
In the leg of a Bengal.
What are you to make
Of these contradictions?
You see a darling on
Charlie, you bow.
She spits out what she'll
Never tell you in
Percent signs and
Full stops.

scorpion

black eyes blink, body snaps back
venomous lust when i sit on your lap
take your pincers, place them exact
make them dance till poison you extract

you chose to get this goddamn close
took those fingers, beckoned me over
so how can it be that you hurt me the most
when we are the furthest apart?

one extraction, this evil transaction
give me poison, then watch what i do with it
let my venom become the ink that fills my pen
injecting paper with floods of bloodied scrawls

you made me cry,
now make me write.
do you see what i've done
with what you did?

you'll expect me to thank you
for drawing it out of me

but don't underestimate my sting
for i didn't do a thing, darling,
this was all you

siren's love song

glass eyed
i bottle these tears
as a maudlin mist swirls
and settles at my waist, gently
kissing my hips and combing
the tips of my salted
curls

together
we watch a temptress
and her teardrops falling into,
becoming, a pearl white selenite
and nothing seems quite so sweet
than to live this desolate life
with this mist by my side and
forever-crying
eyes

a token
of my love, but a product
of my pain, the essence of a
broken soul is the rarest treasure
and so i give it to you. i label
the bottle, tie it with ribbon
and add it to the
rest

i've cried
you so many that from
this rock i see decks of
ships stacked with crates full
of my tears, so full they sink. if
i were to pour them out then the
seas would simply overflow and
pull me back to your shores
where i was sure i belonged
but never again

drink
my potion,
swim in something
deeper than my ocean,
hold this glass just
like you held
me

i want
to be on your
tongue once more, to feel
what you feel, and to fall into,
become, you. you'll take my dose
blindly for the mirrors in my tears
force you to look at your own
reflection and you'll see that
it was you who
put them
there

How can I have fallen in love with all
But none of you? I suppose it is what happens
To the one who wants the candle,
Not the maker.
The banknotes, not the broker.
I lie on a lounge flown in from the Isles,
Lick the Rizla silver I've rolled up on
Its arm. Gorging on riches like a pig.
I wonder why I'm so doe-eyed for you
For no reason, it seems,
And I decide to do everything but
Nothing about it.

wildflower

you admire my petals and they blush at your touch.
a furious fever rises from the surface of their silk
and melts as it finds you.

my buds turn away from your gaze. your dimples
make them shy when you smirk at them like that.
stop playing with my girls.

you lift up the head of my rose and watch my petals
unfurling, swelling, opening for you. not so bad for
a girl who just wants to be wanted. *oh, how it feels
to be chosen.* your ivy fingers wrap around my neck
and i blush a fierce scarlet because it feels just
like those times when—

—you slit my stem and it bleeds sugar. bitter
treacle trickles between your fingers and stings
the cuts left by my thorns. don't try to tame what
belongs to the earth and not you. *you can't handle
such sweetness.*

you toss my carcass into the grass.

i lie, you lied.
we're both a bunch of liars in this wild meadow.

found me at seventeen
lost me soon after
now i dare you to fall in love with me
all over again
let's pretend we're back
in high school
two lovesick fools
with their tender dream
mad fantasy
such a pretty little
unreality
sealed with kisses and
empty promises said by
full babied lips
which loved and loved
and lied

i dare us to try
but you pick truth instead

—*they were such lovely lies*

to be a teenager in love for the first time

we share this nectar between our lips
like a poisoned kiss,
both wrists tied to our false bliss.
i fall at your feet and you leave me there.

this love is like a drug and my god are we
addicted to it. eyes roll back and we overdose.
syrup seeps into our souls, intoxication of liquid
gold, fills us with sweet puffs of smoke, bites the
back of our raw throats. *teenage fantasy.*

it flows like honey in our veins. we drop on
your countertop and our pulses, slow and clumsy
and shy, find each other. they steadily beat
together as they're beating one another. in sync,
in your sink. *overdosed.* well and truly.

dangerous is endangered lust. we both know
we'd die for it. it's euphoric. but we also know
how hard we'll hit the ground when we finally
come down and so we stay up here and let these
ashes fall into our laps. we fall further for
each other. *forever. swear it's forever.*
kiss my neck, just like that, dose me up.
give me more of it. *i said i want more.*

we shared that nectar between our lips.

i fell at your feet and you left me there.

Marie

An off-focus stream of white light shone from the projector above and sparkled with purity, a gentle film of dust clinging to its lens. Seeing this disturbance, a pint-sized man stood up from behind his bench and flew to the rescue, the tail of his dark robe flapping behind him. Superman. From his pocket, he pulled out a handkerchief—an expensive-looking thing with a silk trim—and gave the glass a hurried polish. There was still the unsolved problem of the projector, whose rays were scattered unevenly across the cream-coloured paint of the wall. It was a pretty sight, she thought.

Despite standing on the third step of the staircase that split the courtroom in two, the troublesome projector smirking above him, Mr. Pint-Sized was unable to reach the technical difficulty. He went on tiptoes but did so steadily, as if carrying out this much-needed elevation as slowly as possible would make it any less obvious. His cheeks coloured a furious shade of scarlet and so he angled his face away from the court in a half-hearted attempt to hide them. At the supposed hilarity of it all, there were a few chirps and twitters from the onlookers who sat in the rows below him. Did a hushed voice just suggest they get the poor man a stepladder? The projector was at last within his grasp and he gave it a few rough tugs to fix its position. Et voila.

*

It had been a tiresome journey for Marie Clement, the skies a steel blue and threatening to storm with every passing second. Her carriage pulled into Victoria just after nine, the metal wheels of the half-past eight from London Bridge grinding against the tracks beneath it, fog swirling around its frame. Jagged bolts of brilliant light cut through the sky, sending suit-wearers and luggage-bearers swarming. The Heavens were raging for her. Where was her Marseille when she needed it most? She missed its boat-lined ports and saltwater oysters and navettes flavoured with orange fleur. She missed sipping from little silver glasses of steaming mint tea whilst being kissed by the mistral wind. She missed *home.*

It was this longing that now followed her through the station. She fumbled in her pocket for some loose change and slipped off to the bathroom, pushing through the clusters of tourists who gathered around the turnstiles. Once there, she unbuckled her satchel and pulled out a clear bottle. She unscrewed the cap, brought its salty brim to her lips and drank the vodka straight. She felt its bite and savoured it, then ran her tongue over the cuts of her cracked lips. She was tempted to press down hard on them, draw fresh blood and let the alcohol wash it away. Instead, she gripped onto the ceramic basin and caught sight of her reflection in the dirtied mirror above. Her pale visage was a French meringue, whipped and whirled. One knock and she'd crack. When she lost him, she lost herself, and the alcohol had snuffed out whatever was left. What would Mémère say if she could see her now? That shrill voice rang in her ears. *Un jour, tu deviendras un esclave de tes mauvaises habitudes.* One day, you'll become a slave for your bad habits.

She thought of the sterile hospital; how the coldness of the metal stung as it met her skin. Two of her ribs had been badly shattered, which left great big purple geraniums blooming down her right side. Several fingers had snapped and she'd needed them set, too. It was as if Mattise had blended his plum hues on the canvas of her body, her bones his easel, painting them onto her prickled skin with swift brush strokes.

She soon became an artist herself. In the following days, she spent most of her mornings sitting before the mirror, a box of makeup next to one foot and a can of Red Bull by the other. A dark bruise rested underneath her eye and dispersed into shades of cassis and rouge, its blurred edges kissing the thin shadows cast onto her face by wisps of hair. *That looks painful*, she'd heard all week.

She called home. Her mother was one of Marseille, her French tongue blessing whatever met with it, and Marie craved the soft sweetness she knew so well. But her mother spoke little English and the line had crackled.

"I was in hospital, Mémère."

"The hospital?"

"King's Cross."

"He's angry?"

"Never mind."

To Marie's disappointment, the phone call had lasted just as long as it had taken to dial the number.

How had she managed whilst being all by herself? Loneliness lapped her up like a cat drinking

33

milk. She'd put up with the village tattletales who debated whether Marie's coldness was a result of her divorce or her stereotypically-French brashness. She was the topic of dinner parties and coffee mornings. Oh, how she loved knowing things they did not.

She only trusted Effie, her raven-like wingwoman with the sooty hair and striking red lips. She was rebellious for a lady, and even more so as a lawyer. Her appointment as Marie's representative had been a decision without as much as a choice. They'd spent their teenage years together, but had lost touch since Effie's success stole her to the city. Yet now, even after all these years had passed, Effie had been the first on Marie's doorstop after hearing what had happened, carrying a bottle of Black Absinthe, files full of paperwork and a packet of Marlboro Red. *I'm a lawyer, for God's sake, and a bleeding good one at that. You've already won the battle, Marie. Now prove it.* The thought wrapped its arms around her, kissed her collarbone and soothed her. It did all the things he'd given up doing.

*

Marie had chosen to attend the trial, despite being advised against it. Now, as she sat in the courtroom, watching the slideshow of smoky images projected up onto the wall, it felt like she'd been led into the depths of hell. The red digits of each photo's timestamp flamed against the paleness of her wintery limbs. She felt half-tempted, as her body was digitally enlarged like that, to criticise the stretch marks that tumbled like silver waves over the shore of her stomach, or to insult the angle at which the photographer had taken the picture. She would have liked a wider shot—it would've flattered her better—and none of that overhead lighting. Her eyes were not drawn to the bruises of her battered skin as everyone else's were, but the way her block fringe fell bluntly against her forehead. She'd cut it using dress-making scissors whilst sitting cross-legged in the bathroom sink. He'd commented on it that evening. *You look suspicious. What are you hiding underneath it?* She'd shrugged, letting him lift her out of the basin and take her to bed.

Now, vivid recollections of their failed marriage sprang to mind. That damned night in mid-May. Her wine-stained lips, his musky aftershave, their reignited passion. *I shouldn't have done that*, he'd stuttered afterwards. *We're not meant to do this. We're not together. I don't love you.* His words had stung like drops of a lemon in an open wound. He'd grabbed his keys, flung on his coat, and told her to shut up as she begged for him to stay. She oozed bitter tears.

*

It was hard to take her mind off it when that evening was the reason they were all there. She could hear a tapping—a light scuffle, if that—and wondered if it was his foot drumming a steady beat. He was wedged between two members of his defence, one portly and balding and the other not much different, handcuffs chaining his hands together; those heavy hands, which had spent suns and moons holding her waist and tipping her chin upwards to meet his. She couldn't bear the thought of them tipping someone else's. In her happiest thoughts, she'd pictured him standing in a plastic box, as criminals did in the movies, so that she may imagine pulling out a revolver and putting a bullet in his head, shattering the window into a million shards. She'd only look at him in dreams, not in real life, and so she lolled her gaze, studying the rows of jury members. They were mostly dressed in black, as if they'd all gone through their wardrobes and decided, *yes, I think I'll wear something discreet and slip into the shadows today.* Collectively, they'd achieved quite the opposite. All she could see was a battalion of black-bodied beetles.

She stroked the rough fabric of the chair beneath her and pinched it with nervous fingertips. It reassured her, this touch; it reminded her of Mémère's old lavender cardigan rubbing against her cheek during goodbye hugs. She picked at a loose thread and began to pull, as Effie's bold delivery reached its crescendo. *You went to Miss Clement's house to collect some left-over belongings.* She pulled the thread harder. *You argued and some nasty things were said, weren't they?* She pulled the thread even harder. *You ended up assaulting your estranged wife.* Snap, went the thread.

*

By the time the jury had finished their deliberations and pens stopped scuttling and papers stopped shuffling, suddenly the room was quite— still. The members of the jury sat shoulder to shoulder, like matchsticks lined up in their box, and the foreperson, a wooden man wearing horn-rimmed spectacles and an argyle vest, stood up to speak. All that was required of him were a few syllables, and that was it—some plastic phonetics forced out of his mouth. But it was clear he'd taken this responsibility with such great pressure that his shoulders seemed to be weighed down and Marie feared his bony body might just snap in two.

'We,' he began, 'find the defendant guilty.' *He assaulted me. He assaulted me. He assaulted me.*

If she said it over enough times, she might just believe it. It might just make it true.

And she smiled, because it had worked.

the boy from before

(august 2019)

a boy broke my heart
sometime last summer

he must've not liked
a little sugar in his tea

pink lips like dolly mix
honey hair with buttered tips
or the curve of my waist as
it dipped and he gripped
onto me

he didn't fall for my tricks
ones that make them fall quick
but i know he's missed
tasting me

over breakfasts of toast and jam
when he'd *promise forever*
then sip cups of earl grey
that we'd share together

oh, it was sweet at first but he
couldn't get rid of his thirst
from all the salt he'd drunk
before me

you're not my cup of tea

not one of the girls he could like
i'm far too sickly for his appetite
can't take me on his tongue for
my treacle makes him numb
and he'd rather sip something
with a spoonful of spite

i don't know what i want.
salt or sugar? looks the same,
you decide

never looked me in the eye
when he *promised forever*

now the taste becomes bitter
and nothing's much better
than the heat of this weather

the tragedy of a saudi arabian businessman

has got me into a spot of trouble. i received an email from a mr?—can't be too sure of the name—at quarter past midnight the other evening. he threw about some words, (beneficiary, auditing, and others i don't understand), but he asks for some trust, of which i have plenty, and it's clear that he knows what he's doing. this is strictly confidential, he tells me. our top secret deal. a split of sixty/forty, for a sum of nineteen point three—in millions, i should mention, although i'm used to it now. having to deal with the numbers of these superior transactions.

it started when i read the subject line: to my dear friend. oh, what's this? i'd better have a look— haven't been held dearly for quite a while. he awaits my swift response. (must have me on the mind.) he's been so polite, maybe i just might—no, i won't go there. can't give my heart to a stranger. not this time. and that's when he tells me about

the tragedy of a saudi arabian businessman. motor accident, apparently. can't find any relatives, so i suppose it will have to be me. i sigh, look at myself in my dirtied gown, hair's a mess; biggest concern this week was losing my lip gloss. can't cope with such responsibility. but now that i think about it, i wouldn't mind being an heiress. so i'll give it a shot, do my best. for the sake of the saudi arabian businessman and my new dearest friend.

i pull myself together and type into the internet's search line:

his name
this deal
the sum that is mine

and you'd never guess what i see.

two clicks, four scrolls, and there are hundreds of others who've been given the same offer as *me!* i feel oddly hurt, a little bitter. how can mr(?) have so many dear friends? how greedy can one man be? i need to be his dearest, otherwise my ego, god, it'll feel it, and so i read his love letter over again and—

—oh, i don't believe it.

i suppose i'm no longer his arabian princess. didn't listen when they told me he was dangerous and now he's cheated me like the rest. do they know about me, his other 'dearest friends'?

well, we'll have to split this nineteen point three between us then.

you slip a sunflower seed
into my palm and
tell me to bite

i watch how you crack yours
split it in half then spit out
the shell

will it poison me?
i ask half-sure
the rest of me shy

so you open my lip
with one fingertip and
slip it inside

then tell me to bite
again

no, sweetheart
this love will do that
instead

we're doing it this way now, are we?

playing these games? well, if it's hide and seek you want to play, we must play it properly.

let me hide first. start counting for me. i won't come back for the rest of your life. only once every month just to see if you fancy falling in love with me a second time. making a few more mistakes.

that means it's your turn to seek. come and find me.

please. please. *come and find me*. oh, but give me a little time, make me feel like i'm good at this. like i can do this well. hiding from you. living without you. *but please. please. come and find me!* won't you just come and kiss me quite insane so we can stop playing this pathetic game and *start playing house again?*

—*i said i stopped loving you but that was another lie*

i write this on the day i turn nineteen,
and as i reflect on what my tender life
has been, i realise, as a woman, i live
a life no man will ever have to see. for
this is a man's world, but in a woman's
universe,

and it's been this way since the beginning
of time. femininity spins the earth but seems
to make time stop when the men stop and

stare at the girls on the cusp of womanhood,
close enough to kiss it but not quite; girls
who don't question the wolf whistles,
window taps, smirks when they get a
little closer,

since they've been raised with it. have
learnt to walk a little faster. *show us
a bit more,* they say to her. *she was
asking for it,* they say after that. there's
no going out late, no questioning the men
and their *lusty gaze,*

but tell me why we do not question
the penknives on our keychains; pepper
spray in our perfume bottles; flashlights
for lipsticks;

then tell me why we aren't teaching
the boys that when they grow up we will
not be subjected to their lusty gaze, nor
the ways *they* have been raised in the
first damned place.

misogyny for mothers,
patriarchy for fathers.

clock strikes twelve, girl strikes eighteen,
the men strike on her. the second she's
legal they strip her of protection
and everything else. but those lips
aren't made for kissing. just look at
the magazine makeup smeared on her
dainty doll face

and tell me that legal is just.

—we are not your pretty young things

nemesis

i place the mirror on my window sill,
twist it northeast. first, a sliver of silver,
and then an astral ray, it slices the void
between us and scatters its fair light.

        my spellcraft, your nemesis.

our love eclipsed, so we realigned it
ourselves. *listen. they say we're destined.*

        but now they just whisper.

my poison glitters across the space betwixt
us and catches the sun just like you caught me.
let me go. it pierces through the glass and
beams over rose pink bricks and beige streets,
over the motorways and orbital roads which
led me to you, over little moon-lit lanes with
their sweet oaks, over that roundabout
(you know which).

it finds you uninvited, lets itself in, then
curls up in the corners of your face, those it
knows so well it could trace, stretches and
dozes, softly kissing your nose, and then laps
up the salt of your flesh.

locked eyes, locked hearts, a charm
so sweet it sickens. you say to yourself,

        she's here.

i cling onto you and leave fresh kisses
on your open wounds. it stings us both.
look at me. look at my light. i promise
it'll fix you if you just let it bewitch you.

but our discord is too great. you snap
your blind shut and nothing is left but
the chaos that surrounds and the taste
of my lust's sugar on your lips from
when you had me last.

       night falls but we fall further.

i wait outside your window. you took most
but what's left of me stays. it reflects
not from my mirror, but from my soul,
its compass always pointed northeast,
always towards you.

      always

anything in this world i would do for you.
anything, my love? don't you mean everything?

for everything and more is what you have done
to me. given for free. only you, darling boy,

could twist that knife tongue of yours to the
base of my heart, gouging out gashes you left

seeping when you sank into them last. red-lipped
thief! mining for rubies, thirsty for pools of my

wealth and rich blood! oh, my vlad-like lover with
the sharp white teeth and the pallor of moon, stop

feeding on me! you dress me in gauze like it's a
bloody ball gown then twirl me round silly on our

sickly parquet till i drop at your feet, so lovely and
dizzy. call me manipulative, then kiss me all over!

i don't know much else. i wait for the smacking of
your greedy red lips telling me off till you whisper

ever so softly to the whites of my pretty eyes welled
anything in this world i would do for you.

stop! stop! i don't want you to! for the more you
give me, the more i have to let go of, and

i do not think that is something a girl like me
is able to do with success.

you pinned me down
stitched yourself into my heart
and now you're sewn into my skin
seams running down
my arms, legs, and sides
all the places you ever touched me
everywhere you've been
endless times
running a threadbare love
down to its wires
where my cotton met your cutter
and your hand met my thigh
your fingertips are some
sort of sewing machine
little needle winks at me
with an even littler eye
embroidered
just how you wanted
cross-stitched your surname
at the hem of my collar bone
and whispered feather soft
you belong to me

—you had me tailor-made

glass table girls

look at what they've
become

a product of the wreckage
of love

glass-eyed
tables turned

to the other type of glass

the bottle
saved them from it all

Merlot

Somerset had always been a place of serenity and great beauty.

The days of my youth were joyful. I lived most of my sheltered life on my father's farm, surrounded by the rolling Mendip Hills, with fields of gold and patterns so intricate it was as if they'd been perfectly carved by some divine creator. I'd spend hazy summer days picking lavender and collecting neatly tied bunches in wicker baskets, allowing myself to succumb to the dreamy spell it would cast upon me.

My childhood consisted of churning West Country clotted cream in our dairy, then clambering up apple trees to grab the blissful delicacies they offered. My mother would look on from the kitchen window, a flour-covered apron tied around her hips, with stern warning and concern in her otherwise-mellow eyes. 'Get down from there, right now! I'm warning you, Nicholas,' she'd yell.

It was a surprise to my family when I'd been reluctant to take over the farm and the responsibility it required. Mystery kissed my heart, and I'd spent countless hours clutching the writings of Sherlock Holmes. The pages had darkened with love from the amount of times I'd poured over them, and deep creases trailed across their surfaces. And so, my decision to move to Dulverton and join the police force was one I was convinced was right. Dulverton Police Station had been formed out of the remains of the crumbling town hall, derelict from its former days as the hub of the locals. Its brick walls had seen much of Dulverton's past, from moonlit Viennese waltzes shared between young lovers, to rows of smoke-covered evacuees, who held nothing but their name tags, gas masks and the hope of returning to their city lives. It was quaint, and I was grateful to work there.

'New haircut?' a cheery voice teased one spring morning. In walked Detective Donna Thorpe, a duffle coat slung over her arm and a polystyrene cup of steaming coffee held in her hand. Donna and I had spent most of our childhood days in each other's company. We attended the same primary school, where we'd hide each other's packed lunches and mouth the words to the tiresome assembly hymns when we were less than bothered. We would later come to spend our teenage years sitting in car parks or on wooden benches, drinking stale beer from the cans she'd stolen from her father, as we spoke meaningfully about life in our drunken state and all that it meant. She hadn't changed much since our school days—she was still petite, with a lily-white complexion and a button nose that had a generous scattering of freckles across it. I'd always thought she was pretty.

'Why, do you not like it? The long hair was bothering me,' I responded, a little hurt about her mocking. I thought it looked good. But even with my sore feelings, it was undeniable that her jestful personality was captivating, and drew me towards her even more. I'd already been on a string of dates with a fair-haired farm girl who'd seemed pleasant enough at the time, but after a few weeks, she'd cut all ties. When I questioned what I'd done that was so very wrong, 'All talk, no action' had been the straight-forward response. She blocked my number.

Whilst it stung, I recovered and looked to pursue another relationship—the one between Donna and I.

I could never comprehend my lack of success within relationships. I said what I was meant to say and did what I was meant to do. Was I not good enough? I'd spent many sleepless nights worrying over women who'd never spare a thought for me. Whenever I received a message of refusal, it brought about a misery I could not dispel. I craved an intense connection with somebody and a love that couldn't compare to anything I'd felt before; the feeling of knowing someone was all yours, and you were all theirs.

'Don't worry, Nicholas,' my mother would soothe. 'You'll find her someday.'

To take my mind off my troubles, I threw myself into my work. I still visited my father's farm from time to time, occasionally staying for a glass of sherry; the pair of us would sit by the fireplace like two old chaps, talking, (but normally quarrelling), about various criminal cases and happenings in the town. He was proud of me, I believed, but he rarely showed it. There'd always be a look of longing in his eyes; he wished we could've been working together, me a proper farmer's boy and he my leader, like how it'd been with him and his own father. We both knew this would never happen.

That morning, a few hours after Donna had made fun of my new appearance, she approached me again, this time a stern expression etched on her face. She began to speak. 'We've received an update on a case in the past few minutes. Millie Mortimer. The twenty-one-year-old local. Missing for three days, her body found early this morning. We'll leave shortly for investigation.' Despite this being the only information she gave us, another officer in the room sat up rigidly and straightened his badge. It was the first murder case we'd had in months. For once, petty crimes and paperwork were not at the top of our to-do list.

'I wouldn't wear those to the scene if I were you,' I told Donna, glancing at the patent pumps dangling off her feet. 'It'll be muddy.' She slipped them off, sheer nude hosiery covering her delicate toes. She took out the trainers from the bottom desk of her drawer and turned to speak to me. 'Poor Mrs Carlisle found the body. As you can imagine, just about everyone has heard. You know what happens in a town like Dulverton. These things spread like wildfire.'

We arrived at the scene to be met with tents of white and figures in blue. The ground, already soaked from the spring shower it had endured only hours before, held the imprint of Millie's still body. The heads of daffodils and the other flowers she'd flattened poked out weakly from underneath her limbs, as if they were fighting for air, desperate to escape, but it was clear they'd already lost their battle. As had Millie. She was lying face down, a pair of flesh-coloured tights wrapped tightly around her neck. The garment looked like a pretty pussy bow, hanging from her neck like that. As if she'd been tied up like the ribbon of a present. But whose?

Her fingertips were a cool blue and looked as if someone had dipped them in ice, one by one. And her face, although deathly white, seemed rather peaceful—the plump skin of her faded cheeks was angelic, as if she'd already reached the realm of the dead. Millie the Cherub. A cold chill licked up my spine. How could someone so tortured look so tranquil? Even lifeless, she radiated an innocence and sense of purity I'd never seen in a person before. Her risqué outfit somehow didn't suit her blunt, bitten nails and the friendship bracelets that adorned her dirtied wrists. The silk of her drenched silver dress clung to her skin like it was the paper that wrapped the gift. During the hours that followed, tears were shed, deep-felt sympathies were expressed and the missing posters were ripped off the walls by those who'd spent hours pinning them there.

Murder was on everyone's lips. The town had lost one of its own.

'We need to visit the Half Moon,' Donna explained to me once we'd returned to the station, her dark brows furrowing with concentration as she read the words of the current report. 'Her mother told me she'd gone there to meet someone and had called before the end of the night, asking to be picked up. She couldn't hear Millie's voice well— the pub was busy. But she'd wanted to leave.' The tips of Donna's chestnut hair danced lightly on the notes in front of us, her manicured fingertips flicking through their glossy pages. Her determination was tempting.

We finished writing up the daily report until our shift ended. As Donna was about to stand, I caught her bare arm and plucked up the courage to ask her what I'd been waiting to all month. I'd rehearsed my lines a few times that morning in the mirror, cringing at my stupidity. The expression, the tone, the gestures. I had it all planned out. I'd even called my mother beforehand and asked for her advice. I had to get it over with; the quicker I said it, the sooner I'd know my fate. 'Look, Donna, would you like to get a drink with me at some point? This Friday, perhaps? Just something casual?' I began. My heart raced with the anticipation of it all.

'Oh, of course!' she responded, without a second thought. 'Why don't we invite the others? Make it into some sort of work do? We've not had one of those in ages, you know. Not with how little cash we've got to put towards it. Why don't we have it at your farm? My word, I do miss that peculiar place.' Embarrassed, I agreed, and we said our goodbyes.

The following eve we visited the Half Moon Tavern, which sat opposite the dense woodland where Millie's body was found. It was a cosy inn, filled with men whose Devonshire accents were as strong as the cider they drank. It seemed as if the Dulverton Police Station comprised its most frequent customers—Sam O'Donnell, the washed-up landlord, rang up on countless occasions to complain of drunken brawls between lodgers, or property that had been damaged. And once we'd arrive, (with slight reluctance, it has to be said), he'd never hesitate to slide a beer across the smoked counter, sending us a cheeky wink as he did so. '"On duty" never meant no drinking,' he'd guffaw.

'Detective Inspector Nicholas Slade,' he said the minute he saw us, accompanied by a toothy smile. 'Always a pleasure to see you.' He offered his coarse and calloused hand, which I shook dutifully. The tips of his stumpy fingers had blackened from the amount of cigarettes he smoked.

'You too, Mr O'Donnell—only I wish it was in better circumstances,' I responded, before asking him a few questions. It seemed those around us were oblivious to the fact that a dead body had been found a mere one hundred metres from them, as whiskey was poured and memories with old chums were exchanged.

Sam took his rugged grey beard between his fingers and stared wistfully at the wall. 'I remember seeing that girl,' he started. 'She was with a man. Couldn't tell you who. Never saw his face. They ordered a bottle of Merlot and hid away at one of the corner tables. They left at around eleven. I wish I could give you more, but I was behind the bar all evening. Drinking, not just serving!'

The footage Sam O'Donnell handed over confirmed this. It was evident the monitor in the tavern's back room hadn't been used for a while and it cranked and whirred slowly to awakening. *Tick. Tick. Tick.* On the tape appeared Millie's slight frame in its slinky dress, the sheen of her nude tights catching the yellow glint of the dimly lit lantern hung up outside.

Then, we saw him—a tall figure draped in a black cape-like coat was following closely behind her, his dark hair brushing against his collar. The hem of his coat reached the ground, and when he stepped towards her, it swept across the flagstone. After what appeared to be some brief conversation, Millie was forcefully ushered into the woodland, governed by the large hand that rested on her back. That was it. She was never seen again.

Upon this startling discovery, Sam O'Donnell gasped inwardly. Although he might try, no amount of whiskey could have softened the truth. Donna shot me a sharp look I'd seen before. Whenever her jades became electrified, it meant she was onto something. 'She must've rejected him,' she said as she drove us back to the station. 'He killed her. I know it, Nicholas. It all adds up. Wherever he is, we'll find him. You can't hide in Dulverton.'

I glanced at her momentarily. Her reddened lips were parted, ready to fire out her next declaration. Her hands were gripped onto the steering wheel, her nails digging into the leather that covered it.

I couldn't for one second imagine what she'd do when she found out I was the man she was looking for.

endgame

red carpets bleed down staircases ceiling-high
black checkered tiles kissing corners of white

calling for the match ready for the game ready
for the suitors the jesters the revelry of it all

she spies from her square soft pawns quick
moves coarse calculus white knights captured

chests pushed backs stabbed dames plummet
cracked skulls spilt blood pools of pretty red

screams of traitor betrayal heads roll *get off my
floor!* be gone, charles i, it's not your court anymore

checkmate

they hold onto clock hands and pull time back
as they're on their way down

lock the rest in towers swallow the keys spit
out the capitalism this bleeding game is over

my face worshipped yours
for you were the light
it thought i needed,

to shower my petals
with sunbaked kisses,

keep them fed for this season
and beyond.

but now that it's over,

our love wilting,
        clipped,

we have no choice but to
watch our dying seeds

fall,
        fall like the incessant
crescents eclipsing

in our sun-stolen skies,

weeping as we remember
dusks bedded in the long grass,
slow budding in the rushes,
under jaded leaves to
cover the loving

of two shameful
flowers
who lost their becoming.

mad girl

oh, how we spun
on those
crazed days of craving
a spent out love

when crazy for you
turned into just crazy

and you made me your
mad girl

oh, how i love you!

crazier still

till the days seemed
lightning-quick

lickety-split
spinning long after
you left

forget those ditsy dreams
stitched into your
heavy head

*i will go a little psycho
for you one day*

what i should've whispered
instead

i want the boys in the diners with
the stars in their eyes, a sparkle to
match my own

i want the boys in the diners to
feed peach tarts to my silly little heart,
served with whipped cream and
a love that never leaves

you've nothing left to give me

but just watch how helplessly
i come back to your dull-eyed soul
and cowardly love

every single time

for to be loved
is to be with
you.

—*i'm sick of this temporary love*

I

There comes a time in a woman's
life when the matter becomes too much.
Too much to handle. Too much even for
the *steady, capable hands* of a man
to hold.

And so she collapses. Couldn't take
the pressure. Core orient-cast. Supernova.
Her remnants soar with the nightbirds,
dance in the afterglow, and settle at
the line where dawn slips into
dusk's silk dress.

An outward projection of flat-out
rejection from the men
who tried to fix her
in her own sky.

II

But then comes the gold and the silver,
the providers and the life-givers, the
oxygen to breathe being into her
daughters.

Venus and her femmes tuck moonflowers
in hair, dust puffs of starlit powder over
cheeks, admire curves of celestial bodies,
watch the ways they drip as
they dip limbs into
pools of milk.

III

They wait for the men who wait for them
in the interstellar, spitting cherry pips into
sunsets, rubbing hands with snarling lips,
tearing through the plum of night, ripping
into stolen flesh.

There are plenty of sisters in the sky. Beds
full of them, studded, observed from afar,
wrapped in astral blankets, strewn in
silver sheets.

The men play with them, shatter them,
give the girls too much matter until they
fall just like their mothers.

IV

But then comes the gold.

—*It's a Man's World in a Woman's Universe*

charlotte l oakeby

the falling, the becoming

the becoming

the falling, the becoming

i fell in love with your words
that was it
transient spells spelt by your lips

now as i write
i fall in love with my own

—*i am the love of my own life*

There's Lipstick on Your Collar

Revised Edition

Previously published in The Haloscope Review, Charlotte, North Carolina, September 2019, and Capsule Stories: Frozen in Time, Clayton, Missouri, January 2020

'There's lipstick on your collar,' I'd told you. Do you remember? Of course you do.

I'd cleaned the whole house that day—just for you. I'd scrubbed the kitchen floor until my knuckles were red raw and bitter fumes of bleach stung the back of my throat. I'd ironed your ties, hung them back up on their silver hooks and polished your leather loafers. An Argentinian steak sat on the table, drizzled with béarnaise sauce, ready and waiting to be devoured. I hoped I'd done enough to please you.

'Is there?' you'd replied, the tone of your voice gradually escalating. E, F-sharp, A-flat.

'Don't worry,' I'd said, forcing a soft smile onto my lips. 'I'll put it in the wash.' I saw your shoulders fall with the relief of knowing you'd gotten away with it—or so you thought. You unbuttoned your shirt, exposing the walnut-coloured skin of your chest and the thick, dark hair that covered it, reminding me of your Turkish heritage if you ever did forget to mention.

Once you handed over that dirtied shirt, I sat cross-legged on the bathroom floor and studied it carefully. I didn't doubt for one second that the offending stain had belonged to some other woman's lips only a few hours before. It was devil red. The colour of roses and romance. Blood and betrayal. Was it Chanel's *Rouge Irrésistible*? Or, perhaps it was Dior's *Désir*? I couldn't tell. Either way, it was a pretty shade. I could picture myself wearing it. If I gave you some hints, would you buy it for me as a birthday present?

'That wasn't lipstick on my collar!' you'd responded. 'Don't worry, my darling. Your eyes are deceiving you! It's just a food stain or some pen marker. Don't be silly now.'

I nodded vigorously. 'Why, of course! I was just messing about.' Then I giggled, stroking your shoulder just how you liked it, glancing into the pupils of your chocolate eyes. They flickered with passion. Or was it panic?

I'd been alert for months, searching for more clues, my radars fully-functioning. I had known for a while, of course. Your golfing weekends away with people I'd never met before and receipts of room service in expensive hotels told me all I needed to know. A cup of black coffee—times two; a fruit platter—to share.

You'd arrive home at quarter-past eight every evening, swing your tailored jacket over the banister and toss your keys on the table. And that was my cue. In I came, enter stage left, an apron tied around my waist, ready to nestle in your arms like the perfect housewife you knew me to be. Then, I'd recite my lines: *How was your day? I missed you lots. Dinner's waiting on the table.* I'd inhale deeply —was that perfume I smelt? Did you notice? Or did you just think I couldn't bear to leave the comfort of your embrace?

I could so vividly remember the first moment

we met as if I were still living and breathing it. 'Come over here and meet my work colleague, Dominic,' said the person who'd taken it upon themselves to play Cupid that night. 'It's good to meet you,' you replied, placing a wet kiss on my powdered cheek. That night, I'd seen you repeat the same routine countless times to every woman present: wide smile, eyes locked, hand offered, lips pouted and gently placed on blushing apples. You knew exactly what you were doing, and so did I. Yet there I was, held in your palm like some sort of doll—*yours*.

'I've got to leave in five minutes, but first, I'll grab my coat and also your phone number,' you announced at the end of the night, with so much confidence it made my heart flutter. I must've impressed you.

I received some strange looks from the other guests once I'd spoken to you, but I put it down to jealousy. Everyone wanted Dominic, the most handsome Turk in London. But now, I understand what they really meant. They were looks of sympathy, or warning, I think—fleeting moments of despair that signified another woman had succumbed to the charms of somebody others had learnt to be wary of. My obliviousness proved to be my first mistake.

Stop. Don't fall for him. Look what he'll do to you, I'd tell myself. *So what?* my internal voice would retort. I had already fallen for you, Dominic, and it was too late to catch myself. Everything was perfect…our beautiful townhouse in Knightsbridge, with wrought iron fences, its buckets of white roses sitting on marble steps, and bundles of your handwritten love letters that I tied up with red ribbon and bows. I was beyond besotted.

Do you remember the argument we had after Jane and Peter's wedding? About you flirting with that tattooed waitress—the one who seemed to be glued to your hip the whole evening, always ready with a tray of fresh cocktails and a pout on her silicone lips? You slapped me around the cheek.

'It's a shame I had to do that, my sweetheart,' you told me the next morning, over steaming black coffee and fresh pastries. 'You must be severely insecure to accuse me of something like that. I had to slap some sense into you.'

Then, I knew. I knew what those strangers had been trying to tell me.

You believe I can cope with it, the lipstick on your collar. All I have to do is sit pretty and do nothing—I'll leave all the doing to you. I'll forget I ever saw a thing.

Or so you think.

winter's sister

she does not feel. she's like
ice these days. arctic heart.
blood moon-cold. lumens
frozen. irises glazed. she
glissades down glossed
shades of slopes that became
home to her suns ago. but
he left long before that
and took her temperature
with him. and now,

she does not feel. cold marble
stinging skin. her only warmth
a rubied lip, bitten, thawed
from loving. a rose sleeping
on a bed of white. she knows
what she wants: frost flirting
with the fire, doubt with desire.
she'll rise up above it, then steal
the lust from it. *that* is all
she wants, since

she does not feel. cracked hearts
can't thaw twice. hers is a pond
cut skin-deep, white whiskers
scarring its surface. bleeding blue.
it was the blades that did it.
skin so iced they tried to
skate on it. for they know

she does not feel. when
she tries to be a little warmer,
winter looks at her with
kitten eyes, laps her up, its
wet nose christens her colder.
won't let go of her.

welcome home,
i've missed you.

bless me. bless my heart.

i truly believed that my first would be my only. that the first one would end up being *the one*. do you know how ridiculous that sounds to me now? i truly believed that a pair of lovesick seventeen year olds would conquer the world. build an empire. because they had promised. and once you promise, you can never go back, right? *dear god, please let me be right.*

i miss looking at the broken people and thinking *you wish you had what we do*. now we have become them. and i feel embarrassed about that.

i miss being naive. having a fresh heart. that smug feeling of thinking i'd escaped a fractured one. not having to look after myself because you'd do it for me. being able to put on that perfume without wanting to drown myself with it. (i'd say i miss wearing all the jewellery you bought me but i threw it into the lake last november.) your touch. the biggest problem we had being whether we got caught or not. feeling the butterflies. i miss feeling anything. *dear god, just let me feel something.* your touch—did i say that already? providing. receiving. being treated well. saying your name.

i miss us, but i don't miss you.

i miss being told that i am loved. that i am beautiful. that i am *chosen*. that i'm your *'forever'*. that you'll never let me live another day without you. i miss truly believing that what one says is more important than what one does. i miss daydreaming about the day you'd propose, right after we finished university and had a little flat on the outskirts but it was close enough to commute from because we'd hand-picked it years before and—i miss trusting promises said by a boy who not once remembered to bring his toothbrush.

Persephone's Daughters

If good girls go to heaven,
        where do the bad ones go?

      For if they are the darlings,
           then who are the darklings?
      It's the devil girls I want to know.

i've heard they're heartless
      a different breed
      nothing like those lonely starlets who loll
           on clouds sipping mead
               weeping tears of mercury

      Tell me more.

      beautifully damned they walk
              hand in hand through the
           arches of obsidian which
      surround them obsolete

      plaiting their hair whilst they
           sit on the stairs that lower
              them into the depths where
           they dance with the flames
    and the flames dance with them

      feasting on venison oozing purple
        drinking goblets of mulberried blood
         sucking on cherries a sweet devil-red
        licking up the syrup of lucent jellies

then off to their chambers where they
      fall upon smoked raven plumes
        mulcibers plummeting and like
     magpies they count their
coins of a day's work

and they dance for each other
     just like their mothers did
       laced legs kick high for those
   watching ravenous dead souls
flirt with the goddesses of the nether

hot steam rises and whistles
  at his girls as they wrap around
     each other like ribbon intertwined
   till their silken skin catches light
 and burns their fires within

It's the devil girls who are having the ball.
    I'd rather be bad than be nothing at all.

nightshade

hold me,
bathe in the light
of my love,

hold my curves
with cunning palms,
thaw your frost eyes
with mine.

give me a love
unpolished,
with softest touch
but dirtier mind,

and it'll come for you,

lamping from my
aurous lips to melt
over yours,

until you taste
my candled soul,
then dip into dusk

deeper than
the genie whispered.

charlotte l oakeby

sweet boy
don't cloud your
sorry little head
with false hope

we both know
i'm irreplaceable

—*finally, we agree*

Take a Bow

Revised Edition

Previously published in The Woven Tale Press, Vol. VIII #3,
Long Island, New York, May 2020

Act One, Scene Two

(Scene takes place at the kitchen table. The clock reads half-past ten. HUSBAND is slumped in his chair, his foot tapping against the flagstone. WIFE lets out a sigh.)

HUSBAND: Come on, Samantha. Don't be like this. You know what? I sometimes ask myself if you even want us to be together. Do you not love me anymore? Is that what it is?

(Takes a long sip of cherry brandy.)

WIFE: Don't be so silly! Of course I love you! What's this spontaneous questioning all about? I do wonder about you sometimes.

(Exits.)

Was I convincing enough?

We were having another argument. You'd come home far too late, complained that your dinner was cold, and been surprised when I'd barked that it wasn't my fault and was, in fact, all yours. And so, I had to play my role in the theatre production that was our marriage. Onstage since 1996. Not coming to the end of its run anytime soon.

I've spent many years of our relationship pretending. Acting. I'm unsure what I'm still doing here, under your fat thumb, but I can't deny I once loved you, somewhere deep—*very deep*—down. So deep I can barely see it these days.

But I can still remember how you'd looked when I first set eyes on you, and oh, what a beautiful illusion it was back then. Tousled hair, sparkling gaze, a smile as smooth as melted butter. Just what you saw on the posters. One of my friends had joked, *what if he ages like an ogre? A frumpy old thing? Happens to the best of them.* I laughed off her teasing.

Turns out, she had the last laugh. After all these years have passed, there are so many things I can't stand about you, I could make a list. So, I'll do just that.

Number one. You're a slob.

'Oh Samantha, what would I do without you?' you say, along with some weak demonstration of affection: the lightest peck on the cheek, a quick brush against the shoulder. I don't reply, as we both know what the answer will be—nothing, that will be it.

If it wasn't for me, you'd still be living in your mother's three-bed bungalow, absorbed in her world of undivided attention and spoilings. You must have the pair of us confused, however, as *I* should not be the one making you cups of Earl Grey, ironing your shirts and cleaning up the dirty trails of destruction you leave around the house. You're like a sixteen-year-old boy. I once found five empty cans of lager behind the sofa.

I dare you to moan one more time about how much you have to do. I ask for your help and I'm hit with an insistent stream of excuses; 'Samantha. You know how busy I am with work! You'll have to do it instead.' Cue the eye roll and the heavy head thrown into unforgiving hands.

On those days you work from home, and I leave you looking gormless in the office, (the slightly-larger-than-a-wardrobe-sized spare bedroom with a collapsible computer desk), the clock hands will crawl around their porcelain face and yet there'll still be no sign of action. No keyboard tapping, no pen clicking, nothing. *Where's he gone?* I question. Then, I realise you've most probably gone to the pub with your mates, the seven of you pottering down the cobblestones of the street in single file, as if you were Snow White's Dwarves. In your matching costumes, (white cotton shirts and sand-coloured chinos), you'd all be chirping merrily as the beer rose to your heads. Which dwarf would you be, do you think? I'd say Dopey. It's my factual opinion.

Number two. Your petty, conformist attempts at being 'manly'.

I notice that *thing* you do and you probably think that I do not. Every Sunday morning, despite it being my only chance to get a wink of sleep, you pull me out from my blanketed nest of bedsheets and off we trot to the hardware store, where you'll strut around with your chest puffed out, as if you're competing against the other males who also see you on that bright Sunday morning and decide they're up for the challenge. Who's carrying the heaviest? The most expensive, perhaps? Oh, look! That burly man in aisle three is managing to balance three planks of timber on his shoulders, carry two pots of emulsion paint in each hand and keep his noisy toddler under control—and he hasn't even got a trolley! Then, you'll lead me to the front of the store where all the lawnmowers are lined up in rows, guiding me to the dearest. And, with a considerably audible voice, you'll announce, 'Samantha, I'm going to buy this three-hundred-and-fifty-pounds supreme high-power lawn mower! There's nothing quite like it. Even Leonard, the lunatic in number eighty-seven, doesn't have one!'

Any middle-aged woman who happens to be within earshot of your boastful declarations will shoot me a look of sympathy, as they know. *They just know.*

Number three. Your arrogance.

Nothing is ever your fault, is it? You make us late leaving the house and before we know it, we've met a thunderstorm en route, and so you'll curse and scream at the heavens above as if believing yourself great enough to tell off Nature. Somewhere up there, she's laughing at you.

It was your birthday last week. After the gifts were passed over and ripped open by those grubby hands, you questioned whether some cards had gotten lost in the post, as you were *certain* you would've received more. The day was filled with the sound of your own voice, which you prized more than any present I could ever give you. I did, however, manage to find it within me to reluctantly hand you over a card, whose message wasn't considered at all and was simply there for the sake of filling the space. *Happy Birthday, from Samantha*, it read. No kisses for you—penned, or otherwise.

It doesn't stop there. 'Did you hear what top deal I managed to secure at the estate agency today?' you declare. *Oh, here we go again*. If I'm honest, my love, I really couldn't care less. Yet you carry on. 'It's my talent, Samantha—that's what it is. It must be awfully difficult for my colleagues, having to be around me all the time. I wouldn't want to make them feel disappointed in their own abilities, you know? Second-guessing their career choices, maybe? My word, I wouldn't want to be responsible for that. It's not my fault they couldn't sell water in a desert.'

Number four. Your mother.

Your mother is a part of our relationship just as much as we are. On occasion, it feels like I see more of her than I do of my own husband. Do you remember the time when she just let herself into the house? I'd come back after having dropped the kids at school, (already drained by the passive-aggressive reminders about the upcoming bake sale), to be met by a pair of pink moccasins tucked neatly underneath the staircase. Every cupboard door was wide-open and sugar granules were scattered over the kitchen tiles. 'Make yourself at home, why don't you,' I muttered through clenched teeth.

'Margaret! I wasn't expecting to see you here,' I exclaimed once I saw her, watching her eyes widen with bewilderment, as if she was surprised to see *me* in my own home. I would've had the fright of my life if I hadn't seen her bony hand dipping in and out of the biscuit tin. Her appetite had seemed to increase over the years, rather than go in the other direction. This was a far cry from her past days as the fussiest senior in England. On our wedding day, she'd requested a vanilla sponge cake, please, as her delicate palate couldn't handle much else.

'Are you enjoying your cup of tea?' I asked, directing a fake smile onto my face as I performed my line. I'd handpicked it from the collection in my mind labelled 'To Say When Your Mother-in-Law Breaks Into The House.' Oddly enough, I hadn't needed to use it up until that point.

She clutched the mug with her wrinkled hands, skin so sheer and veins so visible it looked as if our youngest had scrawled on a piece of paper with blue crayons. She sharply shook her head. 'No. I'm unimpressed, I have to say. It doesn't taste nice at all,' she responded with saltiness, smoothing down her greying bob. And, with a mouthful of Scottish shortbread, she continued, 'perhaps you should pop out and get some new teabags?'

Number five. Your DIY abilities—(or rather, lack of them).

Why you spend so much time in that stupid hardware store, I do not know. You have no purpose in there. Most partners are able to carry out a few basic skills, say changing a light bulb or putting up a shelf. You can barely do either. Even something as simple as painting's a struggle, and I can do it considerably better than you. You'll sit cross-legged on our wooden floor, your gut spilling over the waistband of your paint-spattered joggers, waving your brush around and creating some sort of failed Jackson Pollack over the skirting boards. For the love of God, why don't you use masking tape?

I wouldn't want to embarrass you, of course, but let's remind ourselves of your last 'project', if it can be called that—we both agreed that in future, we would only hire a *professional*, after you attempted to wallpaper the living room and had called for me in what can only be classed as an 'alarmed squeal'. You'd knocked over the bucket of paste and consequently glued your forearm to the table.

Number six. You're stuck up the magic faraway tree.

'Samantha,' you once said as you hovered in the doorway, the mobile phone clutched in your hand buzzing periodically. You'd been speaking to the bank advisor, that was clear. 'I think we need to have a little chat,' you began in a serious tone. 'Now, I promise I'm not going to have a go at you, but it's best we get this sorted. You're taking a lot of money out of our joint account. Why are you spending so much, for crying out loud?'

I stared at you with nothing but pure shock. I yelled. A lot. 'Do you know how much it costs to live? To pay the bills? To buy petrol? To feed us all? No! Of course you don't! You slip off to work, happy to leave me to handle things alone. Maybe if you bothered playing your part in this, things would be different!'

You'd been quiet after that. 'Well, I suppose you're right,' you'd meekly replied. Yes. Yes, I was.

After my 'tellings-off', (which no doubt granted you the control over me you desired for a split second or two), I examined our funds myself— and, with a smile a mix of wickedness and pure satisfaction, wondered how you'd explain yourself once I set the bank statements before your eyes; the statements that told of purchases of gardening gizmos and horse racing bets you'd placed.

Number seven. Your questionable (and ineffective) exercise regime.

Every Saturday morning, without fail, you'll get up at quarter to six to supposedly go to the gym. You dramatically clatter around the house to remind us that yes, you are indeed going to—*the gym.* 'Cool daddies work out,' you always tell our children. 'So, that makes me the coolest dad in the world, doesn't it?'

During the first few months of your recently discovered 'love for exercise', I'd shuffle down the staircase to see packets of protein powder lining the counter, as if it was some sort of attempt to radiate the utmost amount of masculinity you could possibly source from yourself. From the safety of the living room, I'd watch you grimace and pour the shakes down the sink just as quickly as you'd made them.

I eyed you up and down one morning. You were dressed in a fluorescent orange vest and a pair of too-tight shorts. I sometimes question whether you actually arrive at the gym or not. Do you get lost on the way? Where are the washboard abs? The bulky arms? The rippling calves? *I* can't see them— I'm not sure about you. You've looked the same for the past fifteen years, with a band of softness around your middle, and squishy thighs that clap together as if they're greeting each other every time you roll over in bed. My body is in better shape than yours, and that's after having kids. It looks as if you could've given birth to our three children, not I, and you're the one struggling to shift the post-pregnancy pounds.

So, when you ask me such a question as 'do you love me?', I don't quite know what to say. I have two options. I could tell you the blatant truth and ship you out the following morning, with nothing more than a cardboard box filled with your checkered flannels and blunt razor blades, or, I could lie through my teeth and save myself a night of explanation and inevitable bitterness. I choose the latter. The show must go on.

I allow myself to indulge in thoughts of the should-have-beens and what-could-have-beens. I shut my eyes and my imagination runs wild. If only I'd pursued the advances of a past lover, I could be holidaying in Greece with some handsome man, his golden body carved by the gods. Instead, I blink to see you lying horizontally on the sofa, comparable to a log of driftwood, hand hidden in a packet of cheese puffs. I have to smile at my foolishness. What was I thinking?

I always think about leaving, but then I'd imagine what you'd do, how you'd react. Would you be angry? Most probably. There'd be great blubbery tears, followed by a few hard nose blows and stifled wails of desperation. I will have seen you in this vulnerable and inconsolable state before—when your pet tortoise died, for example, or when your football team were knocked out the league. Perhaps it's the only part I half-like about you; your innocence. Wetness. Ability to snap back into your infantile habits. I'll be waiting in the wings, ready to swoop in and take full advantage of your soft state.

I suppose a lot of our problems stem back to me. There. I said it. I know I've been compulsively lying and you're bound to be shocked when you find out. I don't like to call it *lying*, as such, just very slight alterations of the truth—all for your own benefit, of course. Little pretty ivory lies. I wouldn't want to hurt you. Can I do it? Can I walk away? I've been *such* a good actress. We are settled here. What would I tell our children? It'd be a complete bolt out of the blue. Would they want to leave the comfort of their village school? Their jewellery-making clubs? Their strawberry-picking days during the summer months?

I once voiced my concerns about our relationship to my mother. 'If you can find a problem with everything, Samantha,' she began, 'it is likely *you* are the problem.' I took from our brief conversation the understanding that you and I were just going through a rough patch, and that my fiery temper and stubborn ways were to blame for our differences.

Surely I should be allowed to live my life to its full, wined and dined by someone who meets my standards and goes way beyond them; someone who recognises my worth? In your self-obsessed bubble, you're unable to satisfy me—everything has, and always will be, *about you.*

But no. This time, I'm putting myself first. I should take a bow for my excellent performance. Your mother is expecting you this weekend. She's cleared out the spare bedroom for you, and I've left your suitcase at the bottom of the stairs.

I've always been here to pick up your pieces, but who's there to put me back together when I fall apart?

THE END

eyes lead you to the soul but also take you back out

i seemed to think that if i shut my eyes
then maybe it wouldn't seem so bad.
see, you're the only one i'd ever had and
i knew no different. *but i want different.*
because i don't want this.

i used to think your glasses magnified the
apertures of your eyes. just enough, so
that i could slip inside them, kiss your
soul, and read you better. read you like
i read the words i write.

how could i ever forget those glasses?
they always fell off and knocked me
in the face when we lay together and so
you'd fold them neatly, cross their legs,
sit them on the mantelpiece and tell them
to wait there patiently like good girls
until the morning came. then, you'd put
them back on and let me cradle your
green eyes with gentle palms. roll them
in my hands. trace them with my fingertips.
stay still. let me look inside you.
i saw your visions, and saw me in them.
vhs camcorder. white gown. what was
underneath. you'd smile.

one day your green eyes cradled me.
they took my hand, pulled me out of your
soul and said *no, sweet girl. you don't belong*
here. go back home. but the hardest part
about your soul turning blind was realising

i'd never been taken there in
the first place.

it was my own reflection
in your damned glasses.

your eyes led me to your soul,
but took me back to my own.

and that is where i fell in love.

second hand heart

to the next man who has my heart,
please be kind to her. she's been hurt.
you'll see this when you hold her,
between thumb and forefinger, and
her fractures still run deep, bleed a
bitter scarlet, weep poisoned tears.
so cradle her gently, speak to her softly.
don't lie to her. she doesn't like that.
be prepared for the temper, all that
comes with it. *pick me up when
i whimper.* treat her right, spoil
her senseless, and if she bites, she's
only picking fights to check you
still care. *so show me you care.*
one of these days she fears
you'll rip open her wounds
just like the others, spit into those
fractures, sting them with the
lust for another, leave her liquid
on her knees. just how you found her.
*don't lie to me. please don't lie to me.
they always lie. they always—*

a recipe to get him back

ingredients you will need

blood of a lost lover (fresh)
a lock of his hair
three drops of mercury
feather of a clipped dove
one drop of vanilla extract
ten ounces of the icing sugar from your lips
four black dahlias (unstemmed)
essence of a broken soul
vial of scorpion's venom (his extraction)
two grams of stupidity
four biting breakup texts
sprig of lavender, dipped in honey
sprinkle of smashed glass
pinch of salt, just for good measure

method

mix well
simmer gently on a low heat
pour it down the sink
burn the recipe
he is never coming back

medusa's interlude

and so it happens again. the snake swallows its tail
with an itching thirst, a rush of lust, just to feel

something worth feeling. half-hearted words, with a
nip of shy to hide behind kittenish smiles, but when i

flip the coin, am aware of this sin, of what i'm
doing, it feels so good to be enslaved by this endless

cycle i'm in. heartless. no clue whose my heart is,
but it's certainly not yours. still, a second thought

is just one more time i think of you and so the desire
flirts with the doubt and wraps you around my finger

like a parcel tied up with string. never met a boy so
innocent. soppy, those things you were saying. i

looked at your portraits, shrugged and said i suppose
he'll do. if i'm honest, it was just to pass the time;

a keen voice at the end of the line to distract
me from the one before you, who left

loveless and *bit my pretty red heart in two.*
light flirts, heavy flatter—oh, what was there to

matter? nothing more than a little bother to
smother me with a love and desire i could get from

no other. meaningless patter. my ego grew fatter,
greedy, gluttonous, repulsed by your fondness

but more so by the lack of it. could have been you,
or him, or the one after that, so how did this turn into

trying to save something we'd etched into fresh skin
with point three needles and irreversible ink? should

have known better. but the snake has compulsions,
her body convulses and bulges, because she needs it,

this vipered affection. *she needs just to feel
something.* she must learn not to seize such perfect

wrong. must surrender attention. then she will
understand this was just a conversation that went on

four hundred days
too long.

selene

the moon knows my secrets
but she won't tell you a thing,
for it's the madness of this life
i live that keeps my universe
spinning. she dips into my chaos
with silvered fingertips, swirls
it south, clusters of sugared
stars stirred into frothed milk.
pure senseless i melt inside it,
lapped up by my dreams; she
steals them as i sleep, to tease
out the secrets within, so sun
won't see them when he wakes
to watch me. she winks, projects
them onto starry screens, plays
them to her lunar lovers coming,
going, through her phases serene,
mouths watering for their
dearest selene. i bathe in the
cream of her moonstoned lust,
fallen in love with a thief! only
she could play marbles with
my planets like this, flicking
their blushed glass then kissing
us quick back to sleep.
selene knows my secrets.
she won't tell you a thing.

the bad boys
aren't good enough
for me
and it's too bad
the good ones
aren't either

Nyx

She melts waxing crescents
With her tongue

As if they were candles,
Her cunning the flame.

In a dusked coven kissed
By twilight, she mothers
Her magic,

The widow of shadows.

Love is her ritual. She casts
It like a spell.

Lets the incense burn out,
The lover disappears. Then
It's onto the next.

Ghosts of the past haunt her
With lusting ecto eyes,

And some still try to slip inside her
Cauldron, begging for a taste
Of her cruel,

The lipped malevolence
That melted them all.

She swirls her sage wand,
Sets it alight,

Burns it like they once
Burnt her.

solstice of solitude

moonchildren, you and i,

kissing the same breaths,
moving through our own

phases,
            fragile
like fresh hearts,

under the same glass sky.

somehow that thought
soothes me,

it whispers that you
never left;

you're just somewhere
that's not here,

always by
            moonside.

I imagine the next love I have
Will be close to divine,
For I will have fallen
For it again;

Chosen to wish upon the selfish stars
Of this loveless world,
Under the spell of its
Lovesick girl.

And when he comes, he'll be
Some sort of blessing,
Blessed with the brokenness of the
Lovesick in question,

For he'll look past my fractures,
And make them his present,
To seal with white kisses and
Dress with red ribbon,

Till my wounds become blessings,
And I become his beautiful
Broken thing.

*—Aphrodite Whispered My Name and Told Me to
Follow Her*

The Elysium of Love

I'm dreaming of the day you will appear,
Lured by the silver on my lily cheeks,
And with a finger blot these blessèd tears,
Which tumble as your tongue so softly speaks.

Struck by Eros and his fervent aim,
Incensèd spirits gloried up above.
That ardent archer, bright his wingèd flame,
Came forth to douse us with his jewelled love.

Time is frozen, locks me in your gaze,
For thine eyes are the ones that hold my own,
And fore'er it shall be this blessèd way,
Eternal sleep with my Endymion.

O, never leave me! Hold me whilst I cry,
I choose to love you even as I die.

seasons of septembers

do you remember the gentle september
we went to pick sunflowers in that
softly-kissed temperature
when even the weather was not as sweet
nor tender as the blooming
of two backseat lovers who
could never keep their sticky
hands off each other
wanting the nectar
and so we left sunflower seeds scattered
on the seats of my other lover
the ditsy black hatchback you know
how i treasure and they were
such a bother.
remember how i muttered?
still wanting your nectar
they're the only thing i have
left of you so i'll refuse to
get rid of them for suns and
moons and seasons of
septembers
they're scattered
just like us
i find reasons to
keep it
the last of our love

In the Garden of my Love

In the garden of my love, my flowers bloom
Fully, bountifully, eternally.

It's wild, untamed, and grows with fondness new;
Trellises of honeysuckles, the sweetest peas,
And blossomed peach roses, the melbas of dawn,
Have their petal mouths kissed full by honeybees.

The sun's syruped rays candy baby buds,
And flirt with dreams of melting maiden snow,
Which covers dew-slept meadows with damask,
And whispers to the shy buds as they grow.

Sweet faeries dip their slippers, pointe by pointe,
In lucent waters of brooklets flowing fast,
Which tumble down mossed banks of fresh verde,
And fall deep into pools of sugared glass.

Spied upon by foxgloves with purple bells,
Dragonflies hover with jewelled wings and
Sip rosewater from teacups, pure silver,
Then flutter, flit and zip into ferned springs.

The rippled rivulets of each creek kiss
The silken earth with aurorean love,
And cleanse it so it's ready for the step
Of the catnipped wanderer from above.

My olive trees cast wisps of dusky shade,
And arching willows weep into ponds deep,
And so I gather bunches of fresh lavender,
To gently soothe him into pixied sleep.

Toadstools keep the secrets of my forest floor,
Their buttered bonnets worn by pretty fays,
Who'll gossip, babble, then hush when he nears,
And take their tales of twilight to their beds.

The next hopeful will be delivered to me
Tangled in thickets, thistles, and sweet briars,
Doused in the syrup of my ripened plums,
Christened my lover by golden-tongued lyres.

Perhaps he'll gallop through my forests of spruce
On a silver dapple horse, an Arabian,
His lust scorching the tips of their minted leaves,
Gracing my petals with pure radiance.

The wells and springs will swell when they see him,
And cobbled paths lit with lanterns will lead
To my elfin grot, on hillside pleasant,
And to him the following words I must read:

Look at me. Look into my eyes.
I only have one thing of you to ask.
You see my flowers; see the love I grow,
I beg you treat me better than the last!

Till then, I'll rest here, cheeks of ashèd rose,
Fever-dewed, complexion custard-cream,
Needing to be blessed by his amber flame,
Melted pure senseless by that gentleman.

In the garden of my love, my flowers bloom
Fully, bountifully, eternally,

Waiting to be given
To you.

every young girl needs her father.

to be his princess, do no wrong in his eyes,
know a limitless love, forgiven every time,

      and so i tried to find this in you,
make up for the loss of mine.

but a boy cannot father me,
especially not a lover,

and a lover who is younger
than i.

to demand protection from
someone who could not protect
another

      was to make the abandonment
a ritual, a little more grief to get
used to,

      and now, somehow,
i have lost two fathers
in one lifetime.

—*they call it daddy issues*

Shall I compare thee to a tidal wave?
  Thou art more tender and more treasured,
Yet fierce enough to drown all life away,
  Kiss of fury's crest perfectly measured.

Sweet Aquarius, you belong to the world;
  Water-carrier, life-giver, soul-taker,
You pull them close, shower them with pearls,
  Then flood them insane with fair breaker.

How do you carry so much then let it all go?
  Serving, providing, with imber eternal,
The Delphinus who dives into your dazzled flow;
  To have your force is what she yearns for.

Though all is fair in love and war,
  Never has a girl so soft been so powerful.

father

you soft thing,

you listen for the gentle beating of a
pair of ivory wings,
thinking that he never truly
left.

of course he didn't.
he's been with you all along,
fluttering by,

your butterfly.

you have believed softer
things.

care instructions

for a flower to bloom it must be familiar with its soil. must know a little darkness and find some comfort within it. must learn how to sleep alone. must know how to find the light and kiss it. must remember its roots. she belongs to herself and nobody else.

*

she must let them taste her honey. must let them spend some time beside her, sleep with her buds, play with her petals. must let them come but also let them go, knowing they'll be fed by other flowers too. must let the west wind hold her, baptise her with its salt water. must be at peace with all who come and adore her.

*

patience. that is key. she does not become the rose overnight.

*

these are your care instructions. you must follow them carefully. sit in the sunlight. let yourself grow. keep hydrated so that your tears can flow. pull out the weeds, let dying petals fall. let wilt what does not serve you anymore. sow seeds within the cracks of your brokenness, let them blossom into blessings. find the root of your wounds, water them, heal them with lessons. when honeybees settle, then leave, do

not grace them with jealousy. let them rest at your
mouth, kiss the silk of your flower sweet. then let
them go.

*

don't be scared of the fall, you've felt the ground
before. *and now you must bloom.*

i'll teach them
how to love me
by showing them
how i love
myself

—*there are lessons to be learnt*

rules of attraction

you must realise that
what is real
will stay

the honeybees meant
for your leaves
will stay

the butterflies meant
for your petals
will stay

the moths meant
to lust for your light
will stay

the love meant
for your pretty red heart
will stay

Ode to Time

I

O, splendid Time! Where art thou, pixied thief?
   Thou faeried spie, you watchest over me,
To steal the seconds of earthlings who sleep,
   And lock them away for eternity.
Art you Lady Chronos, Mother of Time?
   Do you hide deep within the milky blue?
Thou hast ne'er begun and ne'er will end,
   For there does not exist control as thine.
Protect me, Pixie, with intent so pure,
   O, keep thy seconds and keep me with them!

II

With silver scythe and swan pinions plumed,
   Do you sit atop snow mountains peaked and
Count your lilies when they're unfurling, bloomed,
   As snow buds under silken blankets peep?
Come forth, dear Keeper. Thou art not in sight!
   Sit perched like a dove on frosted throne;
Welcome your daughters, Thallo, Auxo, Carpo,
   To swap the seasons with your sunward dial;
Magick up rays so glossed they make sweet moan,
   Your measured pace a gift, not fast nor slow.

III

Oh, fair Time, in your turning hands I trust;
   Decisions handpicked till my fate is fixed,
Your rulings precise, swift and always just.
   Hold me still; dissolve the space betwixt us,

For I am yours and Pixie, you are mine.
　　　Time to live, Time to love, till Time is gone.
Despite the iced bite of your merciless flight,
　　　No sunrise is more aurous-bright than thine;
You dance with gilded orb and kiss her dawn,
　　　Exchange her for the velvet of dark night.

IV

Ah, happy, happy healer, you curest me,
　　　And fix my love lost soul, its fractures deep.
Blessèd fay, protect my heart now freed,
　　　Relieve me, take these seconds as I weep.
Kiss my tears and spin them into silver,
　　　Stay close as I sit by Father's stone;
You were most cruel and stole him too soon.
　　　Redeem thyself, you wicked Time; for
Too long, wingèd creature, you have flown,
　　　Let the crescent hold you in its moon.

V

My sweet cries fall unheard. They beg no more.
　　　O, save your secrets; save the mystery, too,
But my troubles ease for you surround me complete.
　　　Hide if you must, clock-kissing Pixie,
Just promise you'll keep me from knowing,
　　　Protecting me from your frosted throne
Until you sound my final chime, for
　　　Without your watch, I cannot keep going.
Whate'er you choose for me is set in stone.
　　　My love, sweet love, my dearest Time.

sweet ceres

sweet ceres, sweetest girl.

you prised your buds open
when they weren't ready to
blossom, and

now you wish you could go back,
keep them closed, let them sleep
a little longer, for

they are precious, within
their silken gems hold hidden
treasures, and your

maiden petals were furled, skin
untouched, beautifully
weak and

knowingly naive. you fed him
your nectar so that he
would stay and

he did.

he tasted of clementines, honey,
dewed mornings of may, but

you were not ready for him,
with love too immature,

and now you wish you could've
whispered in your petalled ear,

there is no rush at all.

let your buds be shy, for they will
open when the time is
just right.

aphrodite's looking glass

there's something about her
that keeps them coming back

time and time again to cup
their hands into her

silver waters and sip
from it slow

salt kissing tongues on
her cockle shelled shore

apples blushing like roses
nursed by maiden hues of dawn

reflections thirsty
vanity calls
drink me

until the day they look at her
and fall

in love with
themselves

clementine

upon the honeyed hours of
sticky summer nights
we peeled ourselves off each other
like clementines and lay there,
separate, quite still,
till the memories of it,
of you,
became nothing but seeds.
the aftertaste of
a pipped love
still tipped on our tongues,
begging you to squeeze
a little more of you inside
a little more of me.
your skin was bitter-white
with the softest rind and
just thinking of it splits
my heart into four
segments, diced.
forever bursting with love for
you, my clementine.
we didn't move again
that night and i don't say
we ever will.
upon my lonely reveries
i often think
how sad it is
that you spat me out
so easily;
that you do not see
how sweet
we could've been.

i once read that the pen is the patriarchal instrument of man. that he owns whatever he writes with it. his ink, his words, his women. that is how it goes. but as i write now, i will tell you that i do not own my ink, my words, nor my women. they belong to themselves.

as they should.

—*my pen will never conform to male fantasy*

athena

your body is a temple
you are the goddess
only those blessed
enough to explore
and kiss your treasure
should be worth it
so make them fight

when his raging love
strikes my shield
i hope that it deflects
so that he may love
himself
as much as he loved
me
then he will realise why
my soul is enamoured
but my body armoured
for i cannot take a love
as angry as his
make him feel it
make him feel his own side effects

—i want him to see what he does to me

thimble

i do not cry soft pretty tears
like the soft pretty girls
on the soft silver screens

i cry needles and thorns
a little metal to protect
my leaves

a pretty thimbled heart
my soft silver shield

I know how you loved
Breaking my heart.
Gloried in it, in fact.
Victory danced.

Wore my head on your
Belt and my corpse
On your chest, just to
Show other boys what

You're capable of.
You see what I did to her?
Proud as the action man who
Bedded the Barbie then

Scarpered, half-sorry,
Back to the battlefield where you
Knew she'd be, bleeding and
Broken and begging for mercy.

Brave, brave warrior!
What am I to do with a man-child
As brutal as you?

Put my soul on a stick
And a pole through my
Heart if it makes you feel
Better,

But as I lie here,
Surrendered, I wonder,
Half-sorry,

How can this be called
A war when I'm a battle
You never even fought?
Should've known.

You do not fall upon a broken girl
And claim her defeat to be
Yours.

—*Victories Don't Exist Where There's No War*

hekate

indolent eyes look up,
        you know just what they want.

such a soft girl,
wickedly delicate;

half in love with her,
the rest is not;

beauty of blue rocket,
with even bluer heart;

but you have seen the
        other side to it.

she led you deep inside her,
goddess with golden torch,

and locked you there, eternal,
within her chambers four.

deny her of your love,
        she will give you war.

Artemis

Bleeding rose on a
Battlefield of snow,
Nosed by a wolf with
Wildest heart.

Wet paws pad through
Powdered white,
Hunting for a love
Speared by arrows.

She makes the mouths of
Moons water,
Till falling crescents
Spill ivory light.

The eve whispers in his
Frost-tipped ear that
She will rise again, and
Make them bleed,

Storm girl,
Make them fight.

the rain never stopped

did it?

and now,
the fever has risen again.

you unfold dangerously,
floods of ultraviolet, blooming
petals so perilous;

such a pretty violence!
oh, threaten whatever you
bless, *flower child.*

you always knew it would
end like this, and now
you see it.

but do you feel it?

baby girl! you lived life for
the feeling and *now you feel it!*

you watered yourself
as you wept. just look at
what you have become.

firmly pulled towards the earth's
face as you pull away from his.

a list of reasons why i'm grateful for you

1. you taught me a love i never knew to exist,

2. that a boy can fall in love with me as much as you did.

3. but you taught me to love myself before anyone else, even you,

4. and how to value the beauty of the present, how to kiss each passing second.

5. then you taught me that the truest love comes without question,

6. and that when i have questions, i should leave.

7. but you taught me not to blame myself that i could not—*you did it for me.*

8. you taught me we are young, too young for all this,

9. and so you taught me that what one *does* is more important than what one *says*,

10. because otherwise we'd be married at eighteen with a dog, two kids, a house with a slide instead of a staircase and an olympic trampoline, *for god's sake.*

11. as much as i've refused to learn, you taught me there are some promises one cannot make,

12. so i cannot let it *break me* when we have no choice but to *break them.*

13. next, you taught me that i should not chase, just let it come,

14. but with letting something come, i must also let it go;

15. that includes you, darling boy, and i swear *i am learning to.*

16. forgiven?

17. not quite.

18. though one day i might,

19. for you were of me the breaking,

20. but also the making.

21. *the falling, the becoming.*

the falling, the becoming

author's notes

the stories i write for myself are not confined to these pages. i revise the romanticised tales of my future every now and then. whenever they need a plot twist. the story i wrote for him and i, however, was meant to last a lifetime. a forever-type of love. the love of teenage sweethearts. the exact type of chick lit romance i'd poured over as a young girl; a young girl who dreamt of her prince charming every night, wiped lip gloss stains off the boy band posters on her walls, swooned over firemen and lifeguards (i'll never forget the one who carried me to his hut when i got stung by a weever fish in cornwall). boys on the mind. wanting to be saved by one, i think. the princess of my own fairytale. when i met him, i was convinced he'd saved me, and so i was convinced he was *the one*. it didn't take long to fall head over heels for him. i was already on the floor when he found me.

one publication recently called me a 'brittle teen' and i winced a little when they said it. i'd wanted to avoid clichés in this collection, and i certainly didn't want to tie myself to the cliché of the 'brittle teen', whatever that is. the stereotypical brokenhearted girl. never-ending tears, smashing mirrors with flower vases, wanting him back one second then hating him the next. it's always labelled cliché. overused. unoriginal. there are more heartbreak collections than there have been sunrises. but the character of the stereotypical brokenhearted girl is so 'overused 'and 'unoriginal' because *we've all been her at some point.* no wonder they made her a cliché. she's existed since the beginning of time, and so has heartbreak. we're all truly living the same lives, just through different lenses—if there is shame in being a 'brittle teen', then there must be shame in being simply human. i don't even need to say how ridiculous that sounds.

i've realised that i do not get my heart broken. i break it myself. i make up stories based on people i meet, then i fall in love with what i've created. it's no surprise they feel like they've walked onto a movie set when they enter my life. i'm practically casting them. a fresh script for each lover.

as soon as i sensed our love slipping away, i felt compelled to write. it's what i've always done when my universe seems to shatter. i was very aware, even as i sat there frozen, listening to him sob down the phone, that i'd entered a much darker state of existence. philosophically. it brought us both face to face with the brutality of the human condition. simple, straightforward, but sinister. we crave love. connection. affection. but people come and people go. nothing lasts forever.

in order to close this chapter of my life, i have to write it first. i am still young, but i know that losing him will end up being one of the most painful experiences i'll ever go through. sometimes i still find it hard to walk into a room without collapsing onto the floor in fits of tears. we chose to mess around, making promises as children that as adults we could never fulfil. but i'm trying to find the beauty in it—our naivety. we truly thought we were invincible and i think that's sweet.

it was strange being eighteen. not a child, not quite an adult. childlike dreams with adult intentions. it's being young enough to indulge in your crazy imagination, but old enough to convince yourself you're actually capable of living it. *eighteen is only a few years away from twenty three! which is only a few years away from buying a house! marriage! babies!* we skipped a whole decade in our minds and never even questioned it once because we were two teenagers in love for the first time. it was a beautiful concept. the storytelling of star-crossed lovers. we were lucky enough to share the truest, most sublime love. it was the wrong time.

cancer stole my father when i was thirteen. until recently, i didn't realise just how much his passing has continued to affect me throughout my teenage years. there are many things that a young girl can only get from her father. i lost mine at the most crucial point of my life, just as i was starting to turn into a young woman, but he wasn't there to see it. he couldn't adore me, treat me like a princess, or teach me that i do not need a boy to make me valuable because *i am already so valuable by myself.*

i am like my father in many ways. i've got his temper and his fiery side. i've always been amazed how i become more like him the longer we are apart. but there are still lessons he never had a chance to teach me and there is something so bitterly unfair about that.

when i met *him*, not only did i see a lover, but a makeshift father. someone who could morph into the male figure i've so desperately needed for six years. a boy who could protect me, love me unconditionally, and make me *his* princess instead. now, as i grieve for dad, my first love, and a world i once knew, i'm feeling the full force of the same crippling loss i've met before. somehow, it feels like i have lost two fathers in one lifetime.

writing is my way of seeing, understanding and admiring, rather than despising, my complexities and flaws. *the falling, the becoming* is my journal in which i do this. it follows my discovery of first love and the loss of it—a tender, painful experience many can resonate with. i will not give this pain such power, and so it's important that i consider other topics alongside the heartbreak: grief, loss, femininity and empowerment. writing is my healing. through it, i'm becoming the woman i never would have otherwise. it has given me the comfort of knowing that the alchemy of our two souls is utterly irreplaceable. far away, in some other universe, the two love-struck sweethearts will be living the lives we are unable to live for them. of that i am sure. for now, i'm falling…in love with myself.

about

Charlotte L Oakeby is a nineteen-year-old poet, fiction and freelance writer from the United Kingdom. Ever since she was a little girl, she's had a wild imagination, and, when she wasn't reading, she was conjuring up stories of her own. She was, and always will be, a *Malory Towers* kind of girl. She's forever held this desire to write, pouring out dreamt-up thoughts onto pieces of paper or otherwise. When she first began writing, she had a habit of romanticising the most basic of ideas, desperate to write things in a way that *just sounded pretty*. She's still guilty of this, but in *the falling, the becoming*, she explores the brutality of human nature—without a cover of beauty to pacify the pain and make it *just sound pretty*. Her love for writing truly began after cancer stole her father when she was thirteen. She was a daddy's girl and grief took her in directions she did not want to be heading. She came to understand that crafting is her catharsis, and something she feels destined to do. A passionate and determined girl, Charlotte has much she wants to achieve. She will start an English Literature degree in 2021 and hopes to end up a criminal lawyer (with some writing on the side, she promises). She wrote her first published piece, *Forever Yours, Mr. Carter*, at fifteen. Her work is published/forthcoming in multiple overseas publications, including Cosumnes River Journal (Sacramento, California), Gordon Square Review (Cleveland, Ohio), The Haloscope Review (Charlotte, North Carolina), Capsule Stories (Clayton, Missouri), The Woven Tale Press (Long Island, New York), The Daily Positive (New Zealand), C S Laskin's website Live Write Thrive

(San Francisco, California), The Internet Void and Obsessed with Pipework (Somerset, United Kingdom). She was the recipient of a 2019 Editorial Mentorship with Gordon Square Review and subsequently became 'the youngest writer (they have) published to date.' Her mentor, Laura Walter, is 'confident we're only seeing the beginning of this young writer's career.' She was also told by The New Yorker that there is 'much to admire in (her) work.' *the falling, the becoming* is her debut collection.

thank yous

my dear friends and family—those who have held me close when i've been hurting, those who have reminded me they love me, those who have nursed me like i'm a baby bird, those who are turning me into a heartbreak machine(!), those who have put up with me sending them poems at shocking hours just to see what they think.

mum and will—my best friends. my partners in crime. thank you for loving me unconditionally, putting up with my feistiness, and supporting every single one of my creative endeavours, no matter how crazy. i give you eternal permission to tell me 'we told you so.' next time i'll listen to you—i half-promise.

him—thank you for treating me the way you have. know that i did not write this for you, i wrote it for myself, but you made me see i had it within me. thank you for loving me so beautifully.

dad—my guardian angel. my guiding light. i've never needed you more, dad. where are you when i need you most? i'll do everything i can to make you proud. never stop watching over me, my angel, or helping me find my way through this mad, mad world. i love you always.

the falling, the becoming